HARLEY BROWN

DUANE BRYERS

DON CROWLEY

TOM HILL

BOB KUHN

KEN RILEY

HOWARD TERPNING

THE TUCSON 7

Tisa Rodriguez Sherman
and Robert A. Yassin

essay by Jim Willoughby

with comments by Duane Bryers

TUCSON MUSEUM OF ART 1997

Tucson Museum of Art
140 N. Main Avenue
Tucson, Arizona 85701
© 1997
ISBN #0-911611-10-x

Robert A. Yassin
Executive Director

Design and editing:
Laurie Swanson

Printing:
Arizona Lithographers, Tucson, Arizona

Type Font:
Galliard, Arial

Paper:
Quintessence 100# Cover Dull
Quintessence 100# Text Dull

This exhibition has been made possible, in part,
with funds provided by the Tucson/Pima Arts
Council and the Arizona Commission of the Arts
for general operating support of the Museum.

Lenders to the exhibition:

Mr. and Mrs. Joe Dodson
John and Dixie McLean
Phoenix Art Museum
Rica and Harvey Spivack
Vanier Galleries Inc.

*In addition to the above, a number of
lenders to the exhibition
wish to remain anonymous.*

Major support of this exhibition has been provided by the:
Friends of Western Art and
Arizona Lithographers, Tucson, Arizona

Additional support has been provided by:
Settlers West Gallery, Tucson, Arizona
Stuart & Melody Johnson

Photo: David Boyko

Left to right, standing: Bob Kuhn, Harley Brown, Howard Terpning, Tom Hill, Don Crowley
Seated: Ken Riley, Duane Bryers

FOREWORD and ACKNOWLEDGEMENTS

Since my arrival in Tucson six and half years ago, I have really been amazed that Tucson is home to so many wonderful artists. Over the years I have had the good fortune to come to know many of them. I have frequently asked them, "Why Tucson?" Sometimes the answer has to do with art: "I love the light!" or, "There is a wonderful serenity to the landscape and to the city I love." or "There is a really good art community here, lots of artists and that is important." Sometimes the answer has to do with just plain convenience: "I found myself here twenty years ago, and I just stayed." Whatever, for many artists Tucson is the place to be, and that is quite unique particularly in light of the fact that Tucson hardly has anywhere near the kind of art market of a Scottsdale or Santa Fe.

For Harley Brown, Duane Bryers, Don Crowley, Tom Hill, Bob Kuhn, Ken Riley and Howard Terpning -- whom we affectionately call, The Tucson Seven -- all the above prevail, but with an important emphasis on personal friendship and mutual respect for each other as artists. Duane Bryers, the "elder statesman" of the group, was the first to come out to Tucson arriving from Connecticut in 1958. Tom Hill who came out later, had shared a studio with Dick (Duane's nickname) in the 1950s in New York. Ken Riley also lived in Connecticut, and came first to Tombstone, then to Tucson in 1971. Don Crowley arrived in 1973. Howard Terpning arrived in 1977; he knew Ken Riley, another former resident of Connecticut, back east and met the other artists out here. For many years, Bob Kuhn split his time between Connecticut and Arizona finally settling here permanently in 1995. Harley Brown, the youngest member of the group, and Tom Hill have been friends for two decades, and Brown, too, lived part time in Tucson for many years before settling here permanently in 1994. As artists, with the exception of Harley Brown who trained his eye doing thousands of "fifty-cent quick sketches of people," all the artists had distinguished careers as illustrators and left that world in the 1970s for independent careers painting the American West, coming to the West and Tucson at least in part for inspiration.

This is also a group of genuine friends as well as a group of truly talented artists. Likewise, while their work widely diverges stylistically and in that sense they are not a group such as the French Impressionists, they all share a common artistic point of view. Tom Hill aptly describes this point of view in an article by Jim Willoughby in the March, 1997, issue of *Southwest Art*:

> I guess our common bond is that we are all artists who made our own way. We believe in the old idea that you learn the basics--how to draw--and don't do any pretending. We feel like we've paid our dues and know what we're talking about in an academic sense. We've worked our way up from the bottom.

To this, Howard Terpning adds the following which underscores the closeness of the group and the mutual respect they have for one another:

> Many things have contributed to our closeness. We have mutual respect for each other's work. Our personalities are compatible, and we like to joke about everything. No one sets himself apart, and there's no big ego thing among us.
>
> We also learn from each other. I'm influenced by the freshness of Tom's watercolors, the sensitivity of Don's precision and Ken's great sense of design and color. Harley's enthusiasm, humor and spontaneity comes out in his work; you can't help being drawn to what he does. Dick is so solid in his love of conveying humanity. And Bob Kuhn is the greatest wildlife painter there is--he brings such integrity to everything he does.

Mutual respect, a shared artistic and aesthetic point of view, a dedication to the hard work it takes to make good art, and genuine affection for each other are certainly more than enough to join these artists into an important group. And as a group, regardless of stylistic differences, they have also set a high standard for and had an enormous influence on several generations of younger artists.

Now, while these artists have all been in exhibitions together, they have never shown together before as a group. This is something that this exhibition will change, and it is appropriate that the Tucson Museum of Art will do this and that the exhibition will be installed in the John K. Goodman Pavilion of Western Art.

The idea for the exhibition came by way of a

conversation I had with Jack Goodman. From the earliest thinking about creating the Goodman Pavilion of Western Art, I had hoped to use it especially to showcase the work of the very best Western artists living in our area, something we have not till now done very well.

We also did not have the space to do so. The Museum's exhibition and collecting programs have as a particular focus the art and artist of the Southwest with a special emphasis on Southern Arizona. To this point, the Museum has done a very respectable job of this for contemporary artists of our area, especially with the help of the Stonewall Foundation and its annual support of the "Contemporary Southwest Images" series, but a poor job with regard to living Western artists of our region. That began to change with the opening of the Goodman Pavilion a little more than a year ago; this exhibition will accelerate the process. This is the first in what we plan will be an important series of exhibitions of the work of the best Western and traditional artists living in Arizona and especially Southern Arizona which is home to an outstanding group of them in addition to the Seven. Our plan, too, is to follow up this group exhibition with more in-depth one-person exhibitions of The Tucson Seven and to recognize these important and very talented artists in this way.

I want to take this opportunity to thank Jack Goodman for helping us to launch this exhibition. Indeed, it was Jack who identified the artists and urged them to participate. In this, as in all he does for the Museum, Jack worked very hard to bring the exhibition about and to secure support for it. Jack is not just a great friend of Western Art but a great friend of this Museum. Thanks are hardly enough to acknowledge and recognize all his efforts and support. The wonderful essay by Jim Willoughby about the Tucson Seven which follows

was excerpted from his excellent article which appeared in the March, 1997, issue of *Southwest Art* accompanied by the "Commentaries" about each of the artists by Duane Bryers. I want to thank both Jim and Dick for these contributions to our catalogue, and to extend my deep gratitude to *Southwest Art* and to its Editor-in-Chief, Susan Hallsten McGarry for working with us and allowing us to use this material.

This exhibition is as much the work of my assistant, Tisa Rodriguez Sherman, as anyone. She has worked tirelessly on it and has been in constant communication with the artists coordinating the many details of loans, information about the works, color transparencies for the catalogue and the like, and, as always, has done so with patience and good cheer. We worked closely together in selecting the works for the exhibition, in their installation and on this catalogue for which she also wrote the narrative biographies for each artist; consequently, the wonderful results are because of her efforts and her very good eye. My thanks are hardly enough to express my appreciation, not to mention, dependence, on Tisa.

On staff, too, I would like to thank Laurie Swanson, Director of Public Relations and Marketing, who, in addition to her regular duties was responsible for the wonderful design and editing of this catalogue; Susan Dolan, Registrar, and her assistant Jodi Orndorff, for all their help in arranging for loans, for preparing materials for exhibition and for exhibition labels; and David Longwell, Preparator, for his assistance with the installation.

Thanks are also extended to the Friends of Western Art for their very generous financial support of this exhibition and for all their support of the Museum and its programs. John Davis of

Arizona Lithographers has not only produced a superb catalogue with wonderful color plates, but has also made a generous contribution to its production. As this catalogue clearly indicates, John's superb reputation for the best printing anywhere is richly deserved. I also want to thank Stuart and Melody Johnson of Settler's West Gallery, which handles the work of all the artists, for their contribution to the catalogue. Finally, I want to give my many thanks to those collectors, who, in addition to the artists themselves, have so willingly lent to the exhibition.

While the exhibition contains the kind of work for which each of the artists is famous, we have also included some less familiar works, especially illustrations, to further define their accomplishments and their abilities. The artists responded enthusiastically to our requests, lent generously from their personal collections and have been both a joy and inspiration to work with. It has been our great pleasure, Tisa and mine, to come to know all of them very well in the course of organizing the exhibition. For anybody who knows them, in addition to their talent as artists, they are wonderfully warm people, what my mother would have called, "genuine human beings." It was very easy for us to see why they are such good friends. So we want to give special thanks to them, to Harley, Dick, Don, Tom, Bob, Ken and Howard for their art, for all their help and for this outstanding exhibition. We are very grateful.

Robert A. Yassin
Executive Director

THE TUCSON 7

By Jim Willoughby

The following is excerpted with permission from "Tucson 7," an article appearing in the March, 1997, issue of Southwest Art *magazine. The Tucson Museum of Art is very grateful to* Southwest Art *for allowing us to use this material.*

Combining talent, experience and camaraderie, this unstructured bunch gets together for one reason—fun. Harley Brown, Dick Bryers, Don Crowley, Tom Hill, Bob Kuhn, Ken Riley, Howard Terpning and their wives mingle simply because they like one another. These successful painters migrated to southern Arizona from Canada, Michigan, California, Texas, New York, Missouri and Illinois and will socialize at the drop of a Stetson. Breakfasts, dinners, birthdays, holidays, a lizard crossing the road—any excuse is sufficient to bring them together to laugh or commiserate. They even journey to foreign countries together, most recently to Russia for sketching, painting, visiting museums and raising cain.

While camaraderie is the main reason the Tucson 7 hangs together, there are also similarities in the artists' backgrounds and shared influences that caught the eye of Bob Yassin, director of the Tucson Museum of Art, and Jack Goodman, after whom the museum's western gallery is named. Accordingly, the exhibition *Tucson 7* was organized to showcase not only great art but also a group of artists who represent the generation of painters who left the world of East Coast illustration in the 1970s for new careers painting subjects in the American West and around the world.

Duane Bryers, the elder statesman of the group, was the first to migrate to Tucson from Connecticut in 1958. With a background in commercial art, Bryers came West after a stint creating a syndicated cartoon strip for the U.S. Air Force. Between 1978 and 1980 he and wife Dee purchased land in Sonoita, about 40 miles south of Tucson, where Dick designed and built a home of adobe bricks made from mud that he dug up in their front yard. "I was the first to come here, and they all tagged along," says Bryers.

Tom Hill and his artist wife Barbara, recently moved into a new home in the hills above the historic little town of Tubac. Hill was raised in California and attended Art Center College of Design, Pasadena, CA, and the Art Institute of Chicago, IL, before embarking on jobs as a storyboard and set-design artist, newspaper artist/reporter and freelance illustrator.

"I guess our common bond is that we are all artists who made our own way," says Hill. "We believe in the old idea that you learn the basics—how to draw—and don't do any pretending. We feel like we've paid our dues and know what we're talking about in an academic sense. We've worked our way up from the bottom."

Howard Terpning studied at the Chicago Academy of Fine Art, then spent 25 years as an illustrator working for all the leading publications and the movie industry before moving to Tucson in 1977.

"I knew Ken Riley and Don Crowley when I was working back East," Terpning says. "I met the other guys out here—we've known each other for nearly 20 years now. Many things have contributed to our closeness: We have mutual respect for each other's work. Our personalities are compatible, and we like to joke about everything. No one sets himself apart, and there's no big ego thing among us.

"We also learn from each other. I'm influenced by the freshness of Tom's watercolors, the sensitivity of Don's precision and Ken's great sense of design and color. Harley's enthusiasm, humor and spontaneity come out in his work; you can't help being drawn to what he does. Dick is so solid in his love of conveying humanity. And Bob Kuhn is the greatest wildlife painter there is—he brings such integrity to everything he does."

Unlike his cohorts, Canadian Harley Brown was never an illustrator. Rather, after studying in England and in Calgary, Alberta, he spent his early career doing thousands of 50-cent quick sketches of people in restaurants, pubs and town squares. Like Hill, Brown is an inveterate traveler who teaches workshops at home and abroad. He lived part-time in Tucson for many years before permanently moving here in 1994.

Don Crowley studied at the Art Center College of Design before moving to New York, where he created book covers for children's stories, portraits for Readers Digest and still lifes for a major cruise ship company. In 1973 he saw an exhibit at New York's Hammer Galleries of western portraits by his friend, former illustrator James Bama, who had moved to Wyoming. A year later, Crowley and his wife, Betty Jane, packed their bags for Tucson.

"I'm honored to be showing my work with artists I consider the most talented in the world," says Crowley. "They all have finely tuned senses of humor and are very knowledgeable. Dick Bryers is so well-educated, as is Harley, who's as gifted a teacher as a painter. Howard Terpning is one of the most talented people I've ever met—in every respect, from technique to ideas. I don't think there's a shred of envy in the whole group. That's one thing that keeps it together."

Trained at Pratt Institute in his hometown of Buffalo, NY, Bob Kuhn illustrated for sporting magazines, books and calendars until 1970, when his youngest child graduated from college. He divided his time between Connecticut and Arizona until 1995, when he and wife Libby moved to Tucson permanently.

Ken Riley trained at the Kansas City Art Institute, Kansas City, MO, and the Art Student's League, New York, NY. Riley lived in Connecticut while illustrating for major magazines such as the *Saturday Evening Post*. In 1971 he moved to Tombstone, AZ, and later to Tucson. Like Terpning, Riley is a history painter who moved West and found a niche among the legends of cavalrymen, explorers and the Southwestern and Plains Indians. "As former illustrators we worked in very demanding jobs where doing your homework about facts and details was critical to the success of your work," Riley says. "Because the job entailed reading and then visualizing a story, it was easy to make the transition to western American art—I just picked up diaries by men like Lewis and Clark or George Catlin and interpreted them."

Riley was one of the founding members of the National Academy of Western Art in the early 1970s. Shortly thereafter, other members of the Tucson 7 exposed their work to a broader audience as a part of the annual exhibitions held at the National Cowboy Hall of Fame in Oklahoma City, OK, until 1994.

"NAWA is where the Tucson 7 expanded the audience for their work," says Stuart Johnson, owner of Settlers West Galleries, which represents all seven artists. Johnson has watched them evolve, some over more than 20 years, and notes that their work has grown in precision, boldness and complexity. "Unlike their illustration days when they were told what to paint, as easel artists they have had to come up with ideas for paintings and reasons to create scenes. Over the years their familiarity with their respective subject matter has allowed them to go beyond storytelling."

Johnson calls the Tucson 7 "the pillars of American art. Without such accomplished painters, American art would be on shaky ground," he says.

Though the Tucson 7 have shown together at Settlers West, they've never appeared together in a museum exhibition until now.

HARLEY BROWN

Harley Brown, Canadian, b.1939
The Genius (detail), 1995, pastel on paper, 37 x 28

HARLEY BROWN

Our gain was Canada's loss. Harley has few, if any, equals in the dexterous handling of pastel, and he couples that with super draftsmanship. Along with a love of teaching, he is an obsessive collector of art books—he has millions, it seems, stacked to the ceiling and spilling from every surface. As if that weren't enough, he's been a movie buff since childhood and can name the actors in almost any film ever produced. He has an infectious laugh that's recognizable from three blocks away and is the world's best audience for any joke. One is not surprised to learn that this enthusiastic lover of life is also an expert honky-tonk piano player. He's easy to know: The minute you meet Harley, he's your friend.
—Duane Bryers

During his three years of formal art training in Calgary, Alberta, and two years of artistic study in London, the Canadian-born painter, Harley Brown (b. 1939), made his living doing "thousands of 50-cent quick sketches of people in restaurants, pubs, and town squares." By definition Brown is not a portraitist--one commissioned to paint likenesses--he specializes in figure studies, particularly heads. The most interesting heads for Brown belong to people of ethnic groups, particularly Native Americans who to the Anglo eye have distinct, somewhat exotic features. Brown believes that some Native Americans have led their lives in such a way that it affects their physiognomy, so that a study of their faces can encompass their whole beings. He says, "To me, the face is truly the center of an individual's universe." Brown and his wife Carol have traveled throughout Alberta and British Columbia, Canada, as well as the Northwest Territories above the Arctic Circle. The Browns have also visited various locations in the American West to gather material for Harley's paintings. He says, "As with so many other artists, I am on a never-ending search for personal technique and approach. Painting grabs you with a lifetime of challenges that absorb most of your everyday activities. In the big picture, it is an unequaled way of life." A member of the Northwest Rendezvous Group and the National Academy of Western Art (NAWA), which has awarded Brown one silver and five gold medals. He also won the Robert Lougheed Award in 1990. Although Brown has made yearly pilgrimages to Arizona, staying for months at a time, it wasn't until 1994 that he adopted Tucson as his permanent home.

Harley Brown, Canadian, b. 1939
Satchmo, 1992, pastel on paper, 12 x 14 1/2
Anonymous loan

Harley Brown, Canadian, b.1939
The Audition, 1996, pastel on paper, 22 x 16

Harley Brown, Canadian, b.1939
The Circle, 1995, pastel on paper, 22 x 16

Harley Brown, Canadian, b.1939
Rosie, 1993, charcoal on paper, 15 1/4 x 12 1/4 (site)
Lent by Rica and Harvey Spivack

Harley Brown, Canadian, b.1939
Self-Portrait, 1996
pastel on paper, 16 x 12

Harley Brown, Canadian, b.1939
Zelda, 1994, conté on paper, 31 x 20

Harley Brown, Canadian, b.1939
Lady of Central Park, 1993, pastel on paper, 22 x 16

DUANE BRYERS

Duane Bryers, American b. 1911
It Hasn't Been Easy, 1996
oil on canvas, 16 x 24

DUANE BRYERS

Duane Bryers, American b. 1911
Self-Portrait, c.1932, oil on canvas, 17 1/2 x 13 1/2

Born in Lakefield Township, Michigan, a remote area of Michigan's Upper Peninsula, Duane Bryers (b. 1911) grew up there and in Virginia, Minnesota. From the small town he was raised in Bryers remembers the spirit of the land and the expressive faces of hard working women, miners and lumberman. Bryers is essentially a self-taught artist having no formal art training, aside from a correspondence course in cartooning. During his boyhood, in a place devoid of real art, Bryers spent hours in the local library studying the old masters and noted American artists in books and reproductions observing their styles, techniques, and their handling of color and form. Having received national recognition in the 1930s for portrait sculptures in ice of George Washington, Abraham Lincoln, Will Rogers, and Amelia Earheart, and winning second prize in a national soap sculpture competition, Bryers was commissioned by his alma mater, Roosevelt High School, to paint a mural depicting the history of iron ore mining in Minnesota's Mesabi Iron Range. The $3,000 Bryers was paid for his painting financed a move to New York City where he was employed as a commercial artist and experienced national success when he won a war poster competition sponsored by the Museum of Modern Art. Bryers spent the next few years of his life serving the U.S. Air Force as a staff artist. He created a popular cartoon strip that was syndicated nationally for a number of years. After the war, Bryers continued to work in the art world creating advertisements, illustrations for magazines, books, and calendars as well as portraiture. "The human condition is my preoccupation--the body, facial language, gestures and attitudes. Every face has a story to tell, and I apply my instincts and talent to reveal it on canvas." Bryers has won numerous awards for his paintings including NAWA's Trustees Gold Medal Award in 1980 and was the 1987 Tucson Festival Artist of the Year. Bryers is a longtime member of the National Academy of Western Art. He has resided in and around Tucson since 1958.

Duane Bryers, American b. 1911
A Day's Work Done, 1992, oil on canvas, 30 x 40

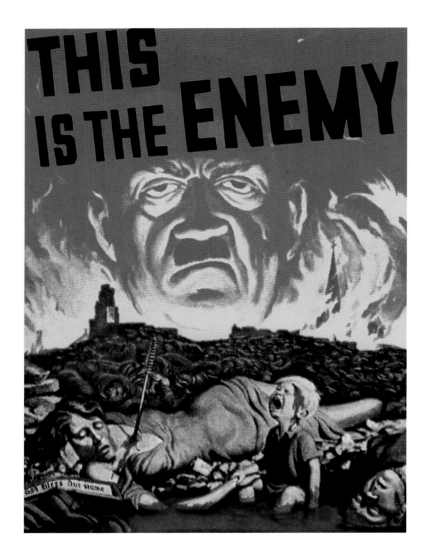

Top: Duane Bryers, American b. 1911
Hilda - Red Underwear with Hat, January/February 1988
opaque watercolor on illustration board, 16 x 12

Duane Bryers, American b. 1911
This Is The Enemy, 1942
laser print, 20 x 16   (winning poster, "Artists for Victory"
national competition, sponsored by Museum of Modern Art, N.Y.)

Duane Bryers, American b. 1911
Cokey, 1945-1951
pen and ink on paper, 6 x 19
(a nationally syndicated comic strip)

Duane Bryers, American b. 1911
Paper Flowers, 1975, oil on canvas, 24 x 36

Duane Bryers, American b. 1911
New Arrivals -- Old Pueblo, 1986, oil on canvas, 30 x 40
(painting for Tucson Festival Society "Artist of the Year" 1987)
Anonymous loan

Duane Bryers, American b. 1911
Portrait of Jeff, 1992, oil on canvas, 20 x 16

Duane Bryers, American b. 1911
Shopping In Lugano, 1984, oil on canvas, 24 x 30

DON CROWLEY

Don Crowley, American b. 1926
Tortillas, 1993, oil, 30 x 40
Lent by Vanier Galleries, Inc.

DON CROWLEY

Don't let Don's cool, laid-back look mislead you. Behind those tight lips and squinty eyes lies a keen and devastating wit. Avoid, if you possibly can, getting to know him too well. Whether you are the recipient of his well-aimed missiles or not, he is always "falling-down funny." He's been particularly hard on me! Always impeccably attired, he moves among us but seems to be from another era. His intriguing home reflects his capriciousness, including his outstanding collections of art deco mementos from the 1920s and '30s. His messy but fascinating studio is another story. That's where he's grim and intensely focused on creating his striking, super-real paintings— mostly of Apache Indians in their colorful beaded garments. His meticulous craftsmanship boggles my mind.—DB

Several weeks after graduating from the Art Center School in 1953 (now the Art Center College) in Los Angeles, Donald Crowley (b. 1926) and his new bride, Betty Jane (B.J.) moved east to New York "where everyone went. That was the goal from the start." For more than twenty years Crowley worked as a commercial illustrator completing assignments creating book covers for children's stories, portraits to accompany articles in *Readers Digest*, and still lifes of the Orient for a major cruise ship operator. In the early '70s a New York gallery featured Western art by James Bama, a former co-worker of Crowley's who had left New York City for Wyoming a few years earlier. Crowley was highly impressed with this exhibition. "It was just a knockout. I couldn't believe the work you could do if left to your own devices." Within a year Crowley was invited to exhibit his own paintings in a gallery in Tucson. Soon after, in 1973, Crowley and his family left the "unbearably pretentious tinsel" of the east coast to make Tucson their home. After relocating to Arizona, Crowley's primary artistic focus was "character studies of the Paiute and Apache Indians." The majority of his paintings portray the surroundings and ideals of Native American societies in the Southwestern United States. In 1994 the artist was elected to the Cowboy Artists of America, which he considers to have been one of the greatest challenges and finest moments in his artistic life. In 1995 the CAA awarded Crowley a gold medal for drawing.

Don Crowley, American b. 1926
The Blue Buckskins, 1990, oil, 30 x 40

Don Crowley, American b. 1926
Seed Corn, 1989, oil, 24 x 20

Don Crowley, American b. 1926
The Purple Shawl, 1996, oil, 30 x 24

Don Crowley, American b. 1926
Light Patterns, 1985, oil, 30 x 24

Don Crowley, American b. 1926
Three Scents, 1991, oil, 14 x 11

Don Crowley, American b. 1926
End as a Saddle, 1989
pencil, 29 x 17

Don Crowley, American b. 1926
The Last Summer - Wyatt Earp, 1989, pencil and pastel, 20 x 16

Don Crowley, American b. 1926
The Pioneer, 1973, pencil, 17 x 23

31

Don Crowley, American b. 1926
The Dressing Tent, 1991, oil, 48 x 60
Lent by Vanier Galleries Inc.

TOM HILL

Tom Hill, American b. 1922
The Alhambra, Granada, Spain, 1984, watercolor, 10 x 14

TOM HILL

Tom and I have been friends since we met in 1951 in Chicago where he was the featured artist for the Chicago Tribune. Our friendship continued throughout our shared-studio days in New York City where we both pursued commercial art careers. Today he enjoys the spectacular new home he designed and built in the foothills overlooking Tubac. Tom is a great architect and has designed and built at least five of his own homes. He is not only one of our most accomplished watercolorists, with workshops around the world and three books to his credit, but a great storyteller as well. He's a masterly and meticulous painter with a polished taboret and every brush in its place—all of which no doubt contribute to the pristine purity of his colorful scenes of Mexican marketplaces and cathedrals.—DB

Born in Texas and raised in California, Tom Hill (b. 1922) was always sure he would be an artist. "When I was six, I would lie on the floor and draw on the backs of discarded envelopes." He attended art school in Los Angeles at the Art Center College of Design on scholarship before continuing his artistic education at the Art Institute of Chicago. Hill has worked as a story board and set design artist for Universal Studios, was employed by the *Chicago Tribune* as an artist-reporter and succeeded in New York as a freelance illustrator and graphic design artist before moving to Arizona to pursue a full-time career in the fine arts. Hill's extensive worldwide travels have inspired numerous watercolors many of which are composed and painted on location. Mexico is of particular interest to Hill. "There's pattern, color, texture, people doing active and interesting things. I've been in more than forty countries, but Mexico happens to be handy and very foreign. I'm not talking so much about the big cities but the little towns, the countryside, where they are still almost in Biblical times as far as the way they do things. It's all very paintable!" Hill has resided in Tucson since 1963 where he has had twenty-one one-man shows. He is a member of the National Academy of Western Art, from which he has won gold and silver medals, and the American Watercolor Society, as well as several regional watercolor groups. In 1994 Hill was elected by his peers a full Academician of the National Academy of Design after being an Associate of this organization for twenty years. He currently lives with his wife Barbara Luebke Hill, who is also an artist, in Tubac, Arizona.

Tom Hill, American b. 1922
In Marrakesh, Morocco, 1990, watercolor, 24 x 38
Lent by Rica and Harvey Spivack

Tom Hill, American b. 1922
Pirates, late 1960s
carbon pencil, acrylic wash, and collage, 12 x 15 (book illustration)

Tom Hill, American b. 1922
Boy Reading a Magazine, late 1960s, carbon pencil,
acrylic wash, and collage, 10 1/2 x 8 (book illustration)

Tom Hill, American b. 1922
Evening Christmas Shopping, Michigan Avenue, Chicago, 1950s
gouache, 20 x 14 (cover for "Graphic" magazine)

Tom Hill, American b. 1922
Fifth Avenue, New York, 1960s, ink, 16 x 13
(illustration for an advertisement)

Tom Hill, American b. 1922
Rocky Point Drydock, 1989, watercolor, 14 x 21

Tom Hill, American b. 1922
Old Italian Hill Town, 1991, watercolor, 29 x 21

Tom Hill, American b. 1922
Western Spring, 1986, watercolor, 20 1/2 x 28

Tom Hill, American b. 1922
The Zocalo, Oaxaca, 1983, watercolor, 21 x 28

BOB KUHN

Bob Kuhn, American b. 1920
April Afternoon, 1988, acrylic, 16 x 20
Anonymous loan

BOB KUHN

After 30 years on their lovely Connecticut farm and a number of years wintering in Tucson, Bob and wife Libby are the most recent to take up permanent residence here. He is considered by many to be America's finest animal artist. With sketch pad and camera, he has made dozens of research trips to Africa and elsewhere and has developed a distinctive style that can be spotted a mile away. After nearly a lifetime of critical observation he has an uncanny understanding of the habits and attitudes of wild animals, and some authorities believe he actually thinks like one! Bob is easy-going, but strong opinions on art and other subjects lurk behind that smiling face, surfacing only when provoked or when the occasion calls for it. He carries no soapbox.—DB

Trained at the Pratt Institute in his hometown of Buffalo, New York, Bob Kuhn (b. 1920) illustrated many books, calendars, and magazines before focusing on easel painting. In 1965 Kuhn had his first one-man show in New York at Abercrombie and Fitch Gallery and sold fifteen of seventeen paintings. In 1970, when his youngest child graduated from college, Kuhn quit illustrating to pursue painting full-time. Many of Kuhn's early paintings are of African wildlife but the majority of his current work features American animals. Kuhn says he doesn't know why he paints animals, explaining, "We were city people, but even as a kid I was drawn to nature and wildlife." Kuhn has traveled extensively to observe his subjects in their natural environments. He has taken eleven trips to Africa, six trips to Alaska, as well as numerous journeys throughout Canada and the western United States. While on location Kuhn sketches and takes notes to refer to when working in the studio. After having selected a subject and gathering references, Kuhn arranges a pleasing composition for the painting. "I like to make arrangements that I control," says Kuhn. "I'm always excited by what an artist does that isn't logical. When I see a painting that shows everything just the way God made it, I yawn loudly and walk away because God already did that job. Pulling off something that isn't expected is what makes a person an artist. When I do a painting that surprises me a bit, that's when I'm really pleased." Kuhn is a member of the National Academy of Western Art and a winner of its prestigious Prix de West in addition to gold and silver medals, and the Society of Animal Artists where his paintings have won five Awards of Merit. He is also an emeritus member of the Boone and Crocket Club. After spending many winters in Tucson, away from their home in Connecticut, Kuhn and his wife, Libby, have recently made Tucson their permanent home.

Bob Kuhn, American b. 1920
Cats Being Kittenish - Ocelots, 1986, acrylic, 14 1/2 x 18 1/2
Lent by John and Dixie McLean

Bob Kuhn, American b. 1920
Lions - study, 1996
conté, 12 1/2 x 14 1/2 (site)

Bob Kuhn, American b. 1920
Big Horn Sheep - study, 1995
conté, 11 1/2 x 15 3/4 (site)

Bob Kuhn, American b. 1920
Rocks, Sabino Canyon, 1985
gouache on illustration board, 10 x 15 1/2

Bob Kuhn, American b. 1920
Old Tree at Kisima Farm, Kenya, 1982
gouache on illustration board, 10 x 14

Bob Kuhn, American b. 1920
A Flap of Vultures, 1978, acrylic, 30 x 60

Bob Kuhn, American b. 1920
Water Babies - Otters, 1987, acrylic, 20 x 30
Anonymous loan

Bob Kuhn, American b. 1920
Cat of Sonora, 1995, acrylic, 20 x 30
Anonymous loan

Bob Kuhn, American b. 1920
Lazy Time, 1990
acrylic, 24 x 32
Anonymous loan.

KEN RILEY

Ken Riley, American b. 1919
Nomads, 1996, oil, 24 x 28
Lent by Rica and Harvey Spivack

KEN RILEY

There's not one among us who wouldn't sell his soul for Ken's magic sense of color and design. In the old New York days, every illustrator eagerly looked forward to Ken's latest work in the Saturday Evening Post. *And so it goes today with his elegant paintings of the Mandan Indians and other historical subjects. Ken is a gentleman through and through, modest to a fault and accepts compliments graciously, then quickly deflects the conversation away from himself. He smiles a lot—the expression on his face in my caricature is pretty standard for Ken Riley. It was only natural that the colorful and historical aspects of Tombstone would lure him away from New York prior to his move to Tucson in 1975. He is now engaged in building a spacious new home in the foothills.—DB*

Born in Missouri and raised in Kansas, Ken Riley (b. 1919) attended the Kansas City Art Institute, his first semester paid for by his high school art teacher. Three years later Riley moved to New York City where he continued his studies at the Art Students League and the Grand Central School of Art. After enlisting in the Coast Guard and serving as a combat artist, Riley returned to the U.S. and quickly found work as an illustrator. Riley's illustrations have appeared in such publications as *National Geographic, Life,* and the *Saturday Evening Post.* Riley began painting the American West while working for the U.S. Forest Service painting Yellowstone and the Grand Tetons. Riley says, "Illustrators are uniquely qualified to paint the history of the West. Their basic training is to take subject matter that no longer exists and give it authenticity--to use their imaginations and empathy to transfer history into a context that becomes very believable." Subjects that are often found in Riley's paintings are the cavalry and American Indians of Arizona. He has lived in Tucson since 1971 and is a member of the National Academy of Western Art and Cowboy Artists of America which has awarded him four gold and two silver medals. He was the Tucson Festival Artist of the Year in 1988 and in 1984 was Artist of the Year of the National Wildlife and Western Society.

Ken Riley, American b. 1919
The Witches Market, Bolivia, 1983
oil, 20 x 40

Ken Riley, American b. 1919
Bodmer Paints the Piegan Chief, 1986, oil, 48 x 40
Lent by the Phoenix Art Museum

Ken Riley, American b. 1919
The Signal, 1984, oil, 22 x 28
Anonymous loan

Ken Riley, American b. 1919
Spring Song, 1989, acrylic and oil, 48 x 38
Anonymous loan

Ken Riley, American b. 1919
The Picket, 1995, oil, 14 1/8 x 10 1/8
Lent by Rica and Harvey Spivack

Ken Riley, American b. 1919
The Basket Weaver, Mexico, 1990, acrylic, 14 x 20

Ken Riley, American b. 1919
Passing Out Orders, 1974, oil, 17 x 36
Anonymous loan.

HOWARD TERPNING

Howard Terpning, American b. 1927
Crow Pipe Ceremony, 1997, oil, 37 x 72

HOWARD TERPNING

Howard went from being a top illustrator in New York to Number One Western Painter in the flick of an eye, so to speak. Study any major painting by Howard and you'll find all the essential ingredients of a masterwork. His paintings of the Plains Indians are thoroughly researched through books, museum artifacts and on-site observation—no flights of fancy here. Howard is a very modest and private kind of guy, genial and warm, and fiercely dedicated to his work. He does smile and laugh a lot—especially during our trip to Russia, where he was at the mercy of Harley and Don. The Terpnings arrived in Tucson 20 years ago and their gracious home has since undergone numerous expansions, the latest being a new studio. There'll be a party soon! —DB

Howard Terpning (b. 1927) was born in Oak Park, Illinois, and as a child lived in Iowa, Missouri, and Texas. After graduating from high school Terpning spent two years in the Marine Corps and upon his return to the United States attended the Chicago Academy of Fine Art on the G.I. Bill. He then served one and a half years as an apprentice to Haddon Sundblom, one of the leading illustrators of the time. Eight years later Terpning moved to the East Coast where he spent twenty-five years as an illustrator working for all of the leading publications and major advertising companies. Among his assignments were designs for movie posters including those for *Dr. Zhivago, Cleopatra,* and *The Sound of Music.* Terpning's fascination with Western lore was untapped when he was commissioned to paint a scene featuring a cowboy pack train for Winchester Arms. Don Crowley, a friend of Terpning's and fellow illustrator, who had moved to Tucson in 1973, urged him to show paintings in a Tucson gallery. Terpning's work was met with immediate acclaim, and in March of 1977 he moved to Tucson with his family to devote himself full-time to fine art. Much of Terpning's artistic work is dedicated to the history of the Western and Plains Indians. "My painting style has remained pretty much the same over the years, but my concentration nowadays is entirely on the Plains Indians. The Native Americans I paint were so much a part of the land, it seems hard for me to portray one without the other. In doing historical paintings, I try to get a good balance between the people and the landscape." Terpning is both a member of the National Academy of Western Art which awarded him a gold medal in 1980 and the Prix de West in 1981, and the Cowboy Artists of America which has awarded him numerous gold and silver medals. One of the highlights of his career was a one-man exhibition at the Gilcrease Museum in 1985.

Howard Terpning, American b. 1927
Blackfeet Head, 1987, oil, 16 x 12

Howard Terpning, American b. 1927
Portrait of Marlies and Steven, 1971, oil, 30 x 24

Howard Terpning, American b. 1927
Portrait of Steven, 1986, oil, 14 x 11

Howard Terpning, American b. 1927
Couple on Boat, 1962, tempera, 29 x 21
(illustration for *Ladies' Home Journal*)

Howard Terpning, American b. 1927
Vietnamese Children, 1969, tempera, 20 x 30

Howard Terpning, American b. 1927
Pipeholder, 1975, oil, 30 x 24

Howard Terpning, American b. 1927
Before the Sunset, 1990, oil, 18 x 24